MY SCARS
TESTIMONIES OF SURVIVAL AND TRIUMPH

MY SCARS
TESTIMONIES OF SURVIVAL AND TRIUMPH

COMPILED BY
MONICA KAYE HARRIS

EXPECTED END

ヨ X

ENTERTAINMENT

Atlanta, GA

Published with assistance from Expected End Entertainment.
ISBN: 978-1-7344101-5-0

Printed in the United States of America

DEDICATION

This book is dedicated to the memory of my mother and grandmother, Burnett Harris Johnson and Katie C. Harris, and to the many people who are suffering from the effects of emotional, mental, spiritual or physical scars.

ACKNOWLEDGEMENTS

I would be remiss if I didn't first acknowledge and thank God for allowing me to be a vessel that He chose for this journey. Thank you to all the wonderful collaborating authors for your willingness to share your transparency and testimonies. Your stories are sure to change the lives of many and give encouragement to those who may have given up.

Thank you to my beautiful daughters, Lakeira Franklin and Ariel Melton, for always being by my side and loving me unconditionally. It is my prayer that through my scars you will be able to maneuver through life with far less wounds than I had to endure. My Scars are your scars. And, to my heartbeat, my grandson Isaiah Lee Melton, I love you. Your pure genuine love for me has been nothing short of amazing and I thank God for you.

To my beloved late grandmother, Katie C. Harris, thank you for raising me to be the woman that I am today. Thank you for your countless hours of prayers. To my late mother, Burnett Harris Johnson, thank you for believing in me. I pray that both of you are smiling down on me and I hope that I am making you proud.

To all the My Scars Ministry Family, my friends, my family and supporters, I appreciate each of you and thank you for taking this journey with me.

Last but definitely not least, I would like to thank my friend, confidant and earth angel, Mr. C. Nathaniel Brown, award-winning author, producer and publisher, for believing in me and giving me the push I needed to get started.

I love you all!

CONTENTS

INTRODUCTION

MONICA KAYE HARRIS

The journey to this anthology began as I was ending an anthology compiled by my friend and professional author, C. Nathaniel Brown. As I was ending my chapter for the anthology, *The American Nightmare: Black Women On Being Black In America*, the Holy Spirit spoke to me in that still small voice and said, "You need to do your own compilation of testimonies and survival stories that have turned into triumph." At first, I was hesitant because the enemy always whispers in your ear when you are destined to do something great or positive. He tries to deter you by putting thoughts into your head, like, "Nobody is going to contribute… You can't write a book… You can't put this together." But I prayed about it and God assured me that this was what He wanted me to do. So, I obeyed and here I am living the vision. After all, the enemy's job is to steal (your vision, your joy and your accomplishments), kill (your dreams, your destiny) and destroy (your dreams, aspirations and even your life) by feeding you lies. We've got to recognize and know that we can do ALL things through Jesus Christ who strengthens us. If God has told us to do something, He will equip us to do what He has envisioned us to do.

I know that we all have scars and many of our scars are not visible to the naked eye. Many of us walk around daily with those scars that nobody can see; those hidden scars that affect us mentally, physically, emotionally, and spiritually. Those scars keep us in bondage like caged birds. We long to escape the pain but don't really know how. We fear that people may look at us differently. We fear embarrassment for ourselves, family or even the church. I am here today to help the caged bird sing. A wound that is not healed leaves a scar that is open to reinfection. But a scar that has healed serves as a reminder that we have overcome.

God knows that I've had my share of scars from birth to now, but to elaborate on all of them would be me completing this entire anthology myself and that is why I am writing it all in my upcoming and much anticipated book detailing the complete story of My Scars. You don't want to miss this long-anticipated book to be released in 2021.

I am here to give you the amazing testimonies of survival and triumph through the lives of five exceptional individuals who have allowed us access into their private lives. They share intimate details about their own struggles and how with God, they survived and are now walking in a triumphant life. Through this anthology, I want people who are going through things in their life to understand that they are not alone. I want them to be confident and know that if God has done it for others, He can do the same for them! This is a book of hope, inspiration, encouragement and faith to show each and every person who picks it up and reads it that God is still in control of the situation, no matter what it may look like. Everyone has a story. Some people, however, are afraid to share their stories. Some feel as though their stories are too grim and contemptible to share. And that is okay. That is why

God has chosen the authors in this anthology to come before you naked and unashamed to encourage others who may be in a similar situation and see no hope in sight.

The Bible states that we overcome by the blood of the lamb and by our testimonies. Our stories and testimonies need to be heard! God delivered us so that we can be encouragement to others and let them know that they too can be triumphant over whatever obstacles they have encountered in life. I wear my scars like battle wounds. If I were in the military, I would say that I've earned more than one Purple Heart. I have been wounded time and time again in this battle called life, but I'm here thanks to the goodness of God! My reward now is being shared with the world through my testimony and through each and every testimony that you will read in this compilation. God truly gets the glory for it all. I know that many times you have heard people say, "You may see my glory, but you don't know my story" and now, these amazing authors and I have decided to share our stories with you so that you can understand what we went through to get to where we are today. I think that God has chosen people whom He allows to go through certain circumstances so He can make and mold them into the person He desires them to be and to use them to help another person going through the same or similar circumstances. When I say this to you, I hope you can understand that I truly believe that I am one of those people. I have been chosen by God to do just what I'm doing. The Word of God in Jeremiah 29:11 says, *"For I know the plans I have for you," declares the Lord, "plans to prosper you and not to harm you, plans to give you a hope and a future."* God knew us before we were formed in our mother's womb. So, if God knew us before we were formed in the womb, don't you think he picked us to be born to a certain person and to go through certain things in life just so He could fulfill the destiny He has set for us? It's kind of like when Jesus had to come to this earth and in a human form to fulfill His destiny. God had already handpicked his earthly mother, Mary, and father, Joseph. Mary was chosen to carry this special anointed child, the Messiah, Our Savior, the one who would come and save the entire world. But He had to go through some horrific things and tumultuous events to get to that point. This is how I feel about each and every one of us. We all must go through some things in order to be a testimony. You can't be a testimony without going through the test.

I believe that I have encountered a little bit of everything relating to the scars of this thing called life. My Scars started when I was born to a 15-year-old single mother. My father was not around. Later, I was told that I was rejected by his family at birth as well. Therefore, I didn't know my paternal side of the family at all. I'm quite sure it was difficult for a 15-year-old runaway little girl to care for herself and a baby. Therefore, I was taken in at six months old and raised by my grandparents. I went through some things with family, rejection, lies, family secrets, etc. You will have to get my upcoming book to understand everything in more detail about the journey I traveled and what I endured.

I finally met my father when I was 16 years old. We bonded and I met a lot of my paternal family members. Three years later in 1989, he died, three weeks before his 40th birthday. The year of 1989 was a hard year for me. My grandfather who raised me died three months before my father did. Then, on top of that, me and my high school sweetheart, the love of my life and father of my daughter had just ended our relationship. I got pregnant and had my daughter my senior year of high school. That was a busy year... I had her in April, turned 18 in May and graduated in June. I did it though. I beat all the odds stacked against me and crushed all of the negative statistics regarding teenage mothers. Now, fast forward to 1992, I'm getting married to my second daughter's father. She was born in 1991. That was a hard relationship, and no one could understand the hidden effects of either of my relationships because I didn't talk about them. I was silent, so everyone thought we were happy. They assumed it was a happy home. But they didn't know what was going on behind closed doors. Never look at someone and envy what they have because you don't know what's going on behind the scenes.

Now, it's 2003 and I decide I need to leave my hometown in Ohio and move to Georgia to start a new life for my children and myself. Two years after I moved, my mother dies at 52 years old and I'm an only child. What a traumatic time that was for me. It hurt and it still hurts. Then in 2006, I meet what I thought was the man of my dreams. We were together for approximately 18 months and he went home with me to Ohio to visit my grandmother who raised me and whom I adored, to surprise her for her 92nd birthday. She told me something at that visit that stuck with me and I knew that it would be the last time I would ever see her alive. My grandmother had Alzheimer's and pancreatic cancer. She passed away January 25, 2008. In honor of her memory, we got married on her birthday December 12, 2008. Don't congratulate me just yet. It didn't go as expected. Let's hit the pedal again and fast forward to May 26, 2009. I had a near fatal car accident and was in Grady Hospital for months and then released to a rehabilitation facility for extensive physical therapy. I was bedridden for months. When I was released from rehab, my husband left me 5 days later. I lost everything!

Let's fast forward again. Now it's 2012 and I have another car accident. My SUV hit a deer, went airborne and flipped three times. My car was totaled, but I walk away with minor bruises and bumps!

These are just a few of my scars that you'll have to read in detail about in my upcoming book. But I believe God had me go through each and every one of those trials so I could be here to help someone else who may be going through. I am a living, walking, breathing testimony of survival and triumph. So, it is my prayer that anyone who reads the stories and testimonies of these triumphant authors will be touched in such a way that they will never doubt the ability of God to pull them through. I pray that this book will increase your faith and you will know that whatever is going on in your life or whatever may be happening at the moment is just a test before the testimony! God will turn the SCARS into stars and travail into triumph!

Enjoy the anthology!

Maya Angelou was one of my favorite poets and writers. Please enjoy this poem as you to begin to enjoy your freedom from the pain of secrets kept too long.

I Know Why the Caged Bird Sings

The free bird leaps
on the back of the wind
and floats downstream
till the current ends
and dips his wings
in the orange sun rays
and dares to claim the sky.

But a bird that stalks
down his narrow cage
can seldom see through
his bars of rage
his wings are clipped and
his feet are tied
so he opens his throat to sing.

The caged bird sings
with fearful trill
of the things unknown
but longed for still
and his tune is heard
on the distant hill for the caged bird
sings of freedom

The free bird thinks of another breeze
and the trade winds soft through the sighing trees
and the fat worms waiting on a dawn-bright lawn
and he names the sky his own.

But a caged bird stands on the grave of dreams
his shadow shouts on a nightmare scream
his wings are clipped and his feet are tied
so he opens his throat to sing

The caged bird sings
with a fearful trill
of things unknown
but longed for still
and his tune is heard
on the distant hill
for the caged bird
sings of freedom.

Monica Kaye Harris resides in metro Atlanta and was born in Mansfield, Ohio. She is CEO and founder of My Scars Ministry, which helps individuals regain their self-esteem and identity after being wounded and scarred mentally, physically, emotionally or spiritually. She also works as an Office Administrator for a Geriatric Psychiatrist specializing in the treatment of Alzheimer's, dementias and mood disorders in the elderly. An ordained pastor and nationally certified chaplain, Pastor Harris serves on numerous organizations as a coach and mentor. She has received many awards of recognition for her commitment to people, including community, ministry, and education. In addition to her ministry work, she enjoys writing, being a print model and acting.

CHAPTER 1

A STORY OF PERSEVERANCE
SONYA WILLIAMS, Ph.D.

On December 1, 2018, I awoke without an alarm as I do every morning. The older I become, the less and less my need for an alarm. I swear that I have an internal alarm clock that is constantly aware of when I need to get out of bed, whether I am leaving for an early morning flight, sleeping in (or trying to) on a weekend or getting up bright-eyed and bushy tailed on a Saturday morning because I'm teaching Zumba. That's right, aside from a being a Ph.D. turned sales executive, I am a certified Zumba instructor. Now, don't get me wrong -- I am not the best dancer in the world. However, I do have the capacity to keep up with the beat and instruct my class to do the same. My students appreciate my upbeat attitude and positive energy more so than my ability to do a body roll.

That chilly morning, my internal alarm clock told me to get up a little earlier because there were one or two song routines that I still had not completely memorized. I popped out of bed and after getting dressed in my super cute leggings and a motivational workout top that read "Good Vibes Here", I went downstairs to my kitchen, ate a bowl of cereal and practiced my routines (in the mirror, of course.) I spent the next half hour smiling at myself while dancing away and just having a good old time...alone! Once I had my routines in order, I drove off to my class which begins promptly at 9 a.m. The gym where I teach is literally seven minutes from my house. I kept thinking, "What a great start to my day!"

It's always difficult to project my dance class attendance.

Therefore, because I am a relatively new instructor with a newly scheduled time slot, I just never know who will show up. In the back of my mind, I thought Mimi (the instructor for whom I was teaching) was going to fire me because my attendance had been super low, like three people. However, on this Saturday, I had eight people in class! Eight!!! My excitement was over the moon! I'm a pretty energetic person by nature, so add eight or so people to the mix and it's a full-on party. Zumba class was so energetic, nothing but high intensity cardio and a lot of fun. All that was missing was the alcohol! Class was conducted as usual, starting with a warm-up, and then followed by a series of fast and moderate songs. My playlist is a nice mix of songs to get your heart rate up and down to burn as many calories as possible. Experts say you can burn anywhere from 350-700 calories from an hour's long Zumba class. There is no doubt that I am on the higher end of the spectrum. I always end the playlist on a slow song and then a cool down, complete with stretching. I felt awesome the entire time of class. However, immediately after class ended, I started to feel this weird pain in my back. It felt like it was trapped underneath my scapula but deeper, as if it was coming from my spine. I started bending over, doing side twists, anything to alleviate the pain, but to no avail. I asked Mimi to beat my back with her palm, hoping the pounding would dull the pain. She did and that seemed to help a little, but when she stopped, I still felt pain. It was as if there was a little man crawling up my spine and he was trying to get out through the crevices of each vertebra. I felt like I had felt this pain before and it normally subsided. But this time, it wouldn't go away.

I went to the bathroom at the gym to put water on my face and tinkle too, but while in the restroom, I gagged. Thoughts started running through my head that I was getting sick, a virus or something. I left the restroom, grabbed my bag and proceeded to my car. I had an errand to run before heading home but decided against it because I could feel my body getting weaker and weaker. So, instead, I drove straight home. As I made the turn into my subdivision, uncontrollable vomit came shooting out of my mouth and into my lap. I thought to myself, "I am really sick! Do I have food poisoning?" I had eaten leftover meatloaf and collard greens for dinner the night before (which means I also ate the same food the night before that). Had I slipped a disc in my back? It was still hurting. Nausea and back pain. I kept wondering, "What in the world could be wrong with me?"

Let me back up. I had plenty of plans that weekend, which included cleaning and decorating the house as my hubby and I were planning to host a huge 'stock the bar/housewarming' party on the following weekend. We bought a home earlier in the year and we wanted to celebrate (finally) with our friends and family. My dear friend, Carla, had attended my Zumba class that morning and followed me home from the gym to help get the house ready for the 50 or so guests we were expecting.

Carla arrived at my house from the gym before I did. So, when I pulled up, I asked her to clean out my car because I was obviously sick. In an attempt not to ruin my car seats, I had pressed my legs real tight together to keep the vomit contained to my clothing. Needless to say, it worked. But my clothes were disgusting.

I entered the house, climbed the stairs and undressed completely in my laundry room. Normally, my workout clothes are pretty soaked with sweat when I leave class. That day, they were also soiled with vomit. I put those clothes in the washing machine and proceeded to my bathroom to shower. I probably should have washed my hair, but my energy was fading fast and my back was still in serious pain.

Because Carla was still at the house, I threw on some clothes and went back downstairs. I was not feeling well at all and my body felt weak. Carla offered to make toast, as I had not eaten since before Zumba class and surely that bowl of cereal was long gone by now. She made toast and brought it over to me. I took one bite and before I could fully swallow that bite, nausea hit me again. Yes, I threw up the one bite of toast. She then offered ginger ale. That too was a no go. At this point, I was vomiting bile because my stomach was completely empty. The pain in my back was still throbbing. Now I am thinking to myself that something isn't right. I turned to Carla and asked her to take me to the Emergency Room. She looked at me a bit stunned. I expressed to her that something was just NOT right and that I thought I should see a doctor. I didn't know exactly what was wrong with me. The same thoughts from earlier started racing through my mind again. Maybe I had food poisoning, maybe I had slipped a disc in my back. Maybe...Maybe... "Just take me to the ER," I pleaded with Carla. "You can drop me off and my dad can pick me up." Before I knew what happened next, Carla dropped me off at the front door of the ER and then went to the parking deck. By this time, I was even more fatigued. I walked up to the counter and literally laid my head on it, too tired to stand on my own. The staff person inquired about the purpose of my visit and I guess I mumbled out my symptoms – back pain, nausea and fatigue. I desperately needed to sit down. Immediately, I was rushed to triage. I then explained that I had taught a Zumba class, and after which started experiencing my current symptoms. I had no earthly idea what was wrong with me. And that's where things got real. Here's what I remember:

The triage nurse takes me back to her ER where I can lie down. Carla walks into the triage area after parking the car. I called my husband, Keith, and my father to let them know where I was. Keith was at work and I tell him not to worry, that I'm fine and that my dad is on his way to the hospital. I ask the nurse for a puke bag because I cannot stop vomiting. A million thoughts are going through my mind: slipped disc, food poisoning, pulmonary embolism (blood clot in the lungs that could be deadly). That last one is a constant worry after a lupus diagnosis years ago. An internal medicine doctor comes into my room. He goes over my history, which includes DVTs (Deep Vein Thrombosis-blood clot in the veins of your legs) and Lupus Nephritis (auto-immune disorder primarily affecting the kidneys). Shamefully, I inform him that I had stopped taking my blood thinner a few months back. I think to myself, "Bad girl! It's definitely a pulmonary embolism (PE)." Oh gosh! How could I be so stupid?! Since I am still having back pain, the doctor begins hitting me on my back which doesn't help or hurt at this point. He asks me to bend my back all different kind of ways. None of these movements affect my back pain. During his assessment, I throw up again. Carla is still at my ER bedside. The doctor draws some blood and leaves without telling me what's wrong.

In the meantime, my father was still on his way. A tech comes to take me down for a chest x-ray. He carts me from the triage areas and when I come back, I see my dad and Carla sitting together and chatting like old friends. Although they had never met before that day, they instantly fell in love with one another, mainly because my father kept telling her how grateful he was that she was there to bring me to the hospital. Carla had plans of her own that day, so I had to make her leave the hospital. She wanted to stay longer, but I told her that I was in good hands and she had done more than enough. A few minutes later, my sweet and nervous husband arrives at the hospital. I was so happy to see him even though I told him that he didn't have to come.

The curtain pulls back and then enters a new doctor, a cardiologist, and his nurse practitioner. Wait. What!? Why is there a cardiologist in my room? He informs me my cardiac enzymes (troponin) are elevated. I asked him what those enzyme levels supposed to be. He said "zero." I asked, "What are mine?" He says, "2.4 ... We are admitting you to the hospital. You probably have myocarditis, an inflammation of the heart. The heart is a muscle and you most likely overworked yours when you were teaching Zumba. So, the plan is to do an angiogram to rule out a blood clot. I really don't think you have a clot, but it must be ruled out. Then, if you don't have a clot, we will perform an MRI of your heart to confirm the myocarditis." I respond calmly, "OK, sounds good but can you please make the vomiting stop? How about some Zofran? Also, they had given me morphine for the back pain which really isn't helping. Not to mention, that I am still extremely fatigued." Next, we wait and wait for either a room, the cardiac unit admission paperwork or a combination of both. Finally, at about 6 p.m., they roll me up to a room on the cardiac floor. My husband and dad are still by my side. I climb into bed and I'm starting to feel a little better. The nausea has finally subsided, but I don't feel like eating. I eat a few spoons of jello and go to sleep.

By the next morning, Sunday, I am feeling much better. I actually have an appetite, but the nurses won't feed me because I have an angiogram scheduled and my stomach needs to be empty for the procedure. Keith arrives and I can tell right away that he's worried but trying not to show it. Around 11:30 a.m., the cardiologist comes into my room. He asked me how I am feeling. I respond positively because I actually feel fine. He says that he will perform the angiogram in the morning. If it is all clear, it will be followed by the MRI to confirm his suspicion of myocarditis. "Wait, you aren't doing an angiogram? The nurses won't allow me to eat because of the procedure!" He looks confused and remarks that they don't perform angiograms on Sundays. I'm STARVING! Remember that I hardly ate anything yesterday and now it's almost noon the following day and my stomach is empty. He orders them to get me food which takes an hour before I finally get a lunch tray from the cafeteria. I scarfed down that food so fast. Surprisingly, the food at the hospital was pretty decent. So, nothing left to do the rest of the day but sit in that hospital room, which was pretty small. The nurses also had me hooked up to a heart monitor 24/7. It was composed of about 4 electrodes plus a monitor, which I stuck in the pocket of my hospital gown. Because of the monitor, I couldn't leave my assigned floor or take a shower. So periodically, I would walk the halls, sometimes alone, sometimes with Keith. The window by the elevators had the best view, where I could see two different expressways merging. It's funny what you find beauty in when you are confined to a small space without many windows. At night, during rush hour, the red and white lights of the expressway were just beautiful! Who knew that the thing I hate the most in life, Atlanta traffic, would bring me the most pleasure during my hospital stay?

Hailey, my extremely smart, adorable and funny 12-year-old daughter, had spent Saturday night with a friend and her father (my ex) had picked her up the next afternoon. I knew I still needed to tell her that I had been admitted to the hospital. The plan was for her spend the rest of the weekend with her Dad; however, she wanted to see me immediately after learning I was in the hospital. She convinced her father not to take her across town to his house; so, he took to one of my friend's house who lived near the hospital. I was so excited to see her late Sunday afternoon. She was put at ease when she saw that I was my normal self and not hooked up to a ton of machines, which was what she had been expecting. I broke the "hospital news" to her over the phone earlier in the day and had told her not to worry, but I think seeing me helped tremendously to ease her fears about the situation.

The angiogram was performed Monday morning. Once again, I had to fast for the procedure. Basically, with the angiogram, the doctor threads a catheter into your femoral artery where dye is inserted to see the arteries around your heart. I lie on the exam table, naked as the day I was born, before they cover me with a large blue paper. The cardiologist begins to perform the procedure and about 10 minutes in, he turns to me and states, "You have a tear in your coronary artery." He immediately stops, takes off his gloves as if he has found what he was looking for. Tears began to flow as they rolled me back to the pre-op room where my husband and father are waiting. I wasn't quite sure what a "tear in my left anterior descending (LAD) artery" meant, but I had a feeling it was severe and serious. I went back up to my room. Keith left for work and my Dad went home.

Tuesday, Wednesday and Thursday brought many visitors to my hospital room. Family and friends stopped by every day to check on me. Some gave me the heads up that they were stopping by and others surprised me. It was the surprise visits that I loved the most! Words can't describe how grateful I was when I would have company. From former co-workers to distant cousins, their visits were the highlight of my day. The best visits of all were, no doubt, from Keith and Hailey. Keith would visit on his way to and from work, twice a day. He spent close to $100 in parking fees, not to mention the money for any and all of my food cravings. I know this event was a scary time for my family, however they never showed it. They were both so strong and held down the home front while I was away.

I had no idea how long I would be stuck in the hospital. In my mind, I was thinking a couple of days. However, I didn't get another visit from the cardiologist until late Wednesday evening. Mind you, I was admitted on Saturday and had the angiogram on Monday. He walks into my room around 7:30 p.m. or 8 p.m. and asks how I'm doing. Let's be clear, I hadn't had any symptoms since my admission. "I feel totally fine. I am ready to go home, get back to work, get back to teaching Zumba, etc..." I then ask him when I could leave so I could get back to my activities. He says to me, "Honey, you had a heart attack!" Wait, what? This is my fourth day here in this hospital and no one, not one person, has ever mentioned the words 'heart attack' to me. What do you mean I've had a heart attack? I thought a heart attack was caused by a clot that blocked the flow of blood. That's not what happened to my heart. Heart attacks were for people who are overweight or unhealthy people who don't exercise. I was/am a certified Zumba instructor. My diet is mostly healthy. I exercise about 4 times a week. There is no way that I had a heart attack and why did you wait until day 4 to say this to me! My heart sank as he said he was keeping me a few more days. Ugh! Additionally, he would perform another angiogram to see if the tear in my LAD was starting to heal. His hope was that the tear would heal on its own without requiring a stent. He would schedule the procedure for Friday morning and if he saw that the tear was starting to heal, then I could finally go home.

Two more days in the hospital. At least there was an end in sight, but jeez, two more days! Two more days without taking a shower. I must really 'stank' at this point. My sanity...oh my sanity. My hospital room felt so very small. Often, I would walk the halls, but they were so short, maybe 30 feet, that walking felt useless. To keep some semblance of normalcy, I would get dressed every day. I refused to keep wearing that hospital gown (except during the night). Many times, I would have visitors and my nurse would enter the room to check vitals, give meds, draw blood and would get confused as to where the patient was! I am 94% sure that I was youngest patient on the cardiac floor. Then on Thursday evening, I was prepped for the angiogram which was planned for Friday morning. As opposed to going through my groin, they decide to go through my wrist this time. Apparently, there is also very large artery there which leads all the way to the heart. The good part about going through my wrist was that I didn't feel so violated. My groin is, as you know, super close to my private parts. A different cardiologist would be performing the procedure and if everything looked good, I would finally be able to go home! (And shower!)

Keith made his usual visit on his way home from work. Hailey was unable to come on Thursday evening due to volleyball practice. She was dying to visit me because it had been a few days since she had seen me. I know her little heart was worried. But I assured her that I'd be home tomorrow (Friday) and hopefully by the time she got home from school. It wasn't what she wanted to hear but she reluctantly said okay.

It's funny, but God works in mysterious ways. The beauty in all of this was that Keith was already scheduled to be off from work the entire next week; so, he could be home to take care of me once I was finally discharged. The second angiogram was as smooth as can be. When I was wheeled into my recovery room, there was my wonderful husband waiting for me. A few minutes later, the cardiologist who performed the procedure appeared and gave us the results. The tear in my LAD was already starting to heal, and in a few hours, I could be discharged and go home.

Following the good news, Keith headed into work and the nurses took me back to my jail cell (I meant room). It took hours but finally I got my discharge papers with a laundry list of new medications. My father came to take me home from the hospital. Hailey made it home from school before I arrived home from the hospital. My promise of already being home by the time she got home from school was not kept, but she didn't seem to care and was super excited to see me.

I am not going to lie. The following weeks were stressful. My official diagnosis was a spontaneous coronary artery dissection (SCAD) which occurred in my Left Anterior Descending artery. First, let's discuss heart disease and the fact that it is the leading cause of death for both African American and Caucasian women! Women who have cardiac events present differently than their male counterparts. The common symptoms of a heart attack normally include pain or chest discomfort, pain in one arm or both, shortness of breath and lightheadedness or nausea. However, my symptoms were back pain, nausea and fatigue. Thank goodness my intuition told me to seek medical attention; however, I never in my wildest dreams imagined that it was my heart causing these symptoms. SCADs are extremely rare and most often occur in healthy women who otherwise have no cardiovascular risk factors. One third of cases occur doing pregnancy or soon after giving birth. While the treatment for heart attacks often involves inserting a stent into the clogged artery, SCAD patients are typically treated with more conservative efforts, such as medication. The risk of reoccurrence is high during the days and weeks following the SCAD event with overall recurring rates around 20%. In researching SCAD patients, many of them have permanent heart damage because they didn't seek medical attention quickly enough or were misdiagnosed when they did. I urge all of you to listen to your bodies and advocate your own medical care.

Although I was discharged from the hospital, I could not work, drive or exercise for weeks. No exercise! That was the worst! I asked if I could take a walk. My doctor said no! The cardiologist put me on bed rest and scheduled a follow up in four weeks. The subsequent days and weeks were spent taking it easy around the house, just longing to get back to my normal routine, but afraid of another SCAD and a hospital stay. At my four week follow up appointment, I just knew that I would be cleared to go back to resuming my normal activities. (I'm an optimist!) I pleaded to go back to work, and he reluctantly obliged, but still no exercise and definitely no Zumba. I was not a happy camper. Can I please go for a walk?! He said yes, but not for exercise. I could basically go out and walk slowly. Ugh!!

Six months later, I was enrolled in cardiac rehabilitation. Cardiac Rehab is a medically supervised exercise program designed to improve your cardiovascular health. There are three facets of cardiac rehab which include monitored exercise, education for heart healthy living and stress reduction. The irony was my heart healthy living was the very reason I had the SCAD. The average age of a SCAD patient is 43 (my age at the time of the event) and usually occurs in fit women who work out. (By no means do I consider myself fit, I eat carbs!) I mean, what's the point of working out consistently and eating right if I will get a heart attack anyway! One good thing about rehab is the opportunity to push my heart rate, while being monitored. It definitely gave me my confidence to get back to exercising. Upon graduation from cardiac rehab, I was allowed to do light to moderate exercise. My heart rate needed to stay in the 150-160 beats per minute range though, regardless of the activity. At least now, I could walk around my neighborhood.

Reflecting on my SCAD/heart attack makes me realize how blessed I truly am to be alive. I'm so grateful for catching it early. I also learned inflammatory diseases like lupus may be a risk factor. Receiving a diagnosis of systemic lupus erythematosus, commonly known as lupus, at the young age of 25 began my journey of perseverance. As if I didn't have enough trials and tribulations in my life with my lupus, Hailey's heart defect and a divorce, the Lord blessed me with a heart attack in my early 40's. Every burden that life has thrown at me has always been considered a blessing because I dig deeper to learn and grow from my experiences. Having lupus forces me to stay in shape. The divorce allowed me to be a better wife to my husband. Hailey's two heart surgeries have given me the strength to teach her how to be strong. I know my faith and positive attitude are the reasons all of my setbacks have been the best setup for my future.

Sonya Goodwin Williams is a fun-loving and optimistic southern girl with a passion for life. Her husband, Keith and daughter, Hailey are the cornerstones of her existence. Her family, both immediate and extended, brings her a sense of pride as it was the village that reared her. Sonya has been an athlete all of her life and loves to play tennis, bike, dance (Zumba) and go on long walks. She strongly believes that everything happens for a reason and uses the adversity in her life as an opportunity for growth. It is because of the hardships in life she has become resilient and heavily relies on her faith for perseverance. By day she is a sales professional in the medical industry, but at heart she hopes to be an inspiration for anyone who has a story to tell. And honestly, it is ALL of us!

CHAPTER 2

GRACE FOR 3
ASHLEY TILLMAN

2018:

"We forgave him long ago", I typed, to this complete stranger, and I meant it. All the while, I was thinking that she didn't even know the half of it, but I was certain that this was the time to express heartfelt forgiveness, so we could finally move forward in life. For 12 long years, we had done everything we could to heal, to deal with the pain, to free ourselves of the burden of everything we had experienced. This woman had no idea what had happened years ago and part of me was irritated that she meddled in our personal lives. I felt a twinge of threat, reminded of all of the struggles we had been through. I felt sick to my stomach at the idea of revisiting wounds we had long since left behind; and then part of me was glad the opportunity had come up to choose to forgive one last time and walk away from it for good. The woman I am emailing is a prison minister/mentor to my ex-husband, who has been convicted of and sentenced to 40 years in prison for abusing our children. While I appreciate her potential intentions of her role, I do not feel the same about her contacting my family and forwarding a letter from their imprisoned father to my now nearly grown boys.

My youngest son, the one far less conflicted from the beginning, seemed somewhat amused by the 9-page letter from his imprisoned father denying he had ever done much more wrong than feed microwave meals, and rush the young children to bed when he was stressed over his lack of income. He laughed and pointed out how crazy and manipulative the letter sounded. To my pleasant surprise, this letter seemed to solidify to my oldest son what he had potentially been struggling with through his teen years and confirm to him all that had happened, versus make him doubt the events of 12 years prior. His quick decision was to use the letter to motivate himself to be a decent, respectable man. I knew we had come a very long way in the 12 years since the unraveling of it all and I couldn't help but feel so grateful and an enormous sense of peace.

Our lives had been tough, but we had learned so much and experienced so much love and grace during the time. I had come to feel genuine peace and appreciation for the process that brought us through it all and to the lives that we came to live. Remembering my dream of living in the exact neighborhood we ended up in; I feel an enormous sense of appreciation and wonder at how different this version is from my original dream including an intact family. I wonder if I would have appreciated it as much, had we not been to hell and back to get here.

1996:

I see him across the courtyard of the campus, and I am intensely drawn to him. His eyes are the brightest blue, illuminated by the Georgia sun. I turn to my friend; "there he is, the guy I'm gonna marry", I say. My friend laughs as we make our way through the sea of people and head to class. I am majoring in psychology, with a minor in criminal justice and dancing at a local club at night to pay my bills through college. It's not that I need to, but it's so much more lucrative than waiting tables or doing normal college jobs; Plus, there's a certain rush I get every night with all that money and chaos surrounding me. My college tuition is covered, so my income is merely for bills, a nice car, cool restaurants and whatever else I want. At this point in my life, I am not yet aware of the possible spiritual implications of my lifestyle. I have yet to learn many things about spiritual attraction and true self love.

"Guess who I saw at the campus gym today?" My friend frequently teases, telling me about his near encounter with my new crush, whose name I am still completely unaware of. I make my friend promise to find a way to befriend this guy and make sure we meet. He's more amused than anything. We have been friends since I began at GSU and he hangs out with me and my best friend pretty regularly. We have never dated, and don't seem to have that level of interest in each other; we are more like brother and sister. He's like the brother I had always longed for.

My own older brother and I had always had a difficult relationship. He grew up splitting time between his father and our mothers' new home with my dad and me. I always felt like he resented me for my "intact family". Apparently, he had been molested by a neighbor of his fathers and was too afraid to tell anyone until years later, when I disclosed his abuse of me to my parents. I struggled with my relationship with my brother; vacillating between undeserved forgiveness and a need to protect myself when others would not. I absolutely loved having guy friends that had my back and had little to no interest in me romantically.

Whether my guy friend helped orchestrate it or not- I finally met this guy, the guy I proclaimed would be my husband one day. We met in a child development psychology class, which seemed sweet at the time, but would later send chills up my spine.

1997 & beyond:

Marcus (that was his name) and I married in March and bought a home in Alpharetta, GA with me dreaming of children and a lucrative career in pharmaceutical sales. While I began pursuing my career goals, Marcus continued college and further education in a master's program. By 1998, I had obtained an amazing opportunity in pharmaceuticals and we decided to start our family. Our first son was born in July of 1999 and we could not have been happier. Our baby was a dream, although I had a bit of a scare during pregnancy and spent 11 weeks on strict bed rest due to "pre-term labor". Shortly after his birth, we decided for Marcus to stay home with our son to keep him healthy, as he kept getting RSV.

More than two years later, Marcus had continued obtaining degrees and certifications and I had done moderately well in my career. We decided to buy a larger home and add our final child. Our second son was born in January of 2003 and I felt our family was complete. Marcus continued staying home; however, I was becoming more and more concerned about his lack of career or any apparent sense of self-worth or enjoyment of life. I would come home from work and the blinds would be closed and there was an enormously heavy feeling in the air. I began dreading coming home. I felt terrible. I was going through a discipleship class at the church where my oldest son and I were recently baptized in, but I felt like I must be a bad mom, because I did not want to go home. I found myself thinking of cheating on my husband, who had no interest in me anymore (I had never cheated on someone in my life) and I was generally uncomfortable with my entire home life. I had been working for an amazing company where I called on psychiatrists and decided to talk with one I had befriended. Although I felt like I was a terrible person and mother, I still couldn't shake the feeling that my only option was to divorce my husband. I felt terrible; riddled with guilt for deciding to tear apart my children's family and home. These feelings of guilt lingered for over a year. This was also a catalyst for me to go on a deep faith journey. It became my time of spiritual growth as well as God using it to prepare me for what was to come.

2006:

I had been divorced for over a year and dating when I did not have my boys, but thoroughly enjoying my half time with them. Due to their young ages, they were in each home every 3-4 days, to reduce how long they were away from each parent.

Marcus had returned to school to obtain his teaching certificate, while substitute teaching and volunteering at the Methodist church on Sundays. I had been chasing after God in a large, non-denominational church that I had loved for years, but was not of interest to Marcus. The kids seemed to enjoy both. Oddly, my youngest son started having extreme separation anxiety. He made me hold him his entire 3rd birthday party, cried and clung to me when I dropped him off at daycare, especially on the days I mentioned his dad picking him up. Marcus, still not having a full-time job, begged for me to pay him to care for the boys instead of paying for childcare. I declined and mentioned to him my discomfort with this idea as well as his "making" our then 6-year-old sleep with him. Marcus rebutted with child psychology course stats on bonding...

In May 2006, after I had done a Relay for Life walk all night; I picked up the boys from their dad and headed to PetSmart with them and our new puppy while our home was being shown to sell. On the way, my oldest son began asking me about God, the Holy Spirit, and how we "listen to God".

"Mom, how do we know if we're obeying God or a person?"

I answered with some sleep deprived version of God speaking to us in our heart.

"Mom, I think I need to tell you something, but I'm scared."

Again, my sleep deprivation answer went something along the lines of: 2 Timothy 1:7. *"For God hath not given us the spirit of fear; but of power, and of love, and of a sound mind."*

So, he began his "imaginary story about a boy" with the same name as him!

What unfolded after this was blur and several months of pieces of sexual, physical and mental abuse being disclosed in court ordered therapy, monthly visits to family court to assess and ultimately continue family protective orders until the forensic interviewers and police had enough to arrest Marcus.

It took 2-plus years to go to trial, which was a partial blessing, as the boys experienced a tremendous amount of healing at church, their small private Christian school and at home. I still was concerned about the impact of "reliving it" to some extent as they were required by law to testify against their dad for all he had done to them. Days 1-4 of the trial went by uneventfully. I survived being on the stand first, along with Marcus' attorneys attempts to hang me for every mistake, indiscretion and thing I had done "wrong" in my life. I truly experienced the essence of: Romans 8:31. "What shall we then say to these things? If God be for us, who can be against us?"

The boys each testified on day 4 and the state rested. We planned to return to our normal schedule and I took the boys to school the next day. Before I left the school, following my time in discussion and prayer with the boys' teachers; I started getting phone calls that Marcus had not shown up to court and they wanted me to stay at the school with a police officer for my and the boys protection. Marcus had removed his ankle monitor and ended up going missing for four years.

During the time he was missing, I kept the boys in private school, kept them and myself plugged into our church groups and did everything I could to continue to move forward. We dealt with life as it came up, clearly still feeling many of the scars from their experiences. I eventually had to tell the boys that Marcus was not in prison, where he'd been sentenced to 40 years in absentia. Life went on for us. The boys played sports, we traveled, and we loved to the best of our ability. Ultimately, Marcus was caught and brought to his rightful prison.

Several years after his capture, some scars were activated by my oldest son's first heartbreak, but by the grace of God, it also led us to my dream home back near the one we lived in as a family of four. We have become a close dream family of three all with clear goals and varying abilities to help others through hard times and to love fiercely and unconditionally, just the way God has loved us.

2020:

Due to the pandemic, this year has been different and odd at times. It has also been a blessing, as the three of us have had a lot of time at home and have thoroughly enjoyed our time together. The next chapter of our lives awaits us as my oldest son is in his second year of college and my youngest will leave next year for college himself. I, without a doubt would remove the pain and hurdles we all had to endure, but I am enormously proud of the young men they have become through all of it. The strong relationship between the 3 of us and my faith in our future could not be better. I am glad that we allowed the experiences to shape us instead of sink us. Jeremiah 29:11 has and will always be a profound verse for the three of us: *"For I know the plans I have for you"*, declares the lord, *"plans to prosper you and not to harm you, plans to give you hope and a future"*.

Ashley Tillman is a medical sales representative in Atlanta, GA, where she grew up and has raised her children. Ashley became a Christian in her 20s. She and her, now adult boys, rescue dogs. She mentors at risk youth and lends a caring ear and support to friends dealing with life struggles. Her words of encouragement to anyone dealing with a painful situation is: Proverbs 3:5-6 – *"Trust in the LORD with all your heart and lean not on your own understanding; in all your ways submit to him, and he will make your paths straight."*

CHAPTER 3

TRAGEDY AND THE LOVE OF GOD
JERRILYN HARRIS

Nurse: Well mom, "There are two!"
Me: "Two what?" (Eyes bucked)
Nurse: "You are having two babies!"
Me: "Oh Lord!" (Head Drops)

On June 30, 1997, I gave birth to Juston who weighed 2 lb. 4 oz. and Jerrion who weighed 2 lb. 12 oz. They were two months early. They were born 27 minutes apart, due to Jerrion trying to come out with his hands first and not his head. The doctor had to push him back inside of me so that he could be born correctly and cause no harm to him or me.

Each baby had their own special care team. After each baby was born, the nurse briefly held them up for me to see them and rubbed their cheeks on mine, but then hurried them away quickly to the NICU. Once awake, I could not wait to go down to the NICU to see my babies. When I arrived to the NICU, Juston, who was my sick baby, had to have oxygen and was on a warm table under a blue light. He was hooked up to all kinds of tubes and lines. Jerrion, who was my well baby, was in an incubator with only a feeding tube and monitors. As I looked down at their perfectly made little bodies, I found myself looking to see what features they had of mine. Juston had a pretty brown complexion with a button nose and Jerrion was of a lighter complexion with hazel eyes, they both had silky straight hair. They were not identical, but they looked like they belonged to each other.

I visited them every hour that I could and stayed the entire time, not wasting one minute. After about a week or so, Juston had to have a blood transfusion. I was told by the doctor that they would have a ten week stay in the hospital and not to expect them before then. I was soon discharged and hated to leave both of them in the hospital, but I continued my regular visits to see them. With each visit I took them some of my home brew what I called "Mamalac" (that's my cute name for breast milk). Before leaving the hospital they both had to weigh at least 4 lbs. and be weaned off of tube feeding and learn to be breast fed. Juston and Jerrion both came home earlier than expected. Jerrion came home first at six weeks and then one week later, Juston came home at seven weeks.

I had gone out to celebrate my birthday, and my mom kept the boys for me. Once home I knew I only had a short time before it would be the boys next feeding time. I had them on the same feeding schedule from the hospital: 5, 9, and 1 around the clock. Like clockwork, I heard Juston crying. It was time to eat! I got up and turned on the light. Jerrion was still sleeping. I went to comfort Juston and gave him his pacifier so that I could run and get bottles made for both of them. As I began to step away from the baby bed, I rubbed Jerrion on his back, thinking to myself that it was odd that he was not crying as well. Then, I stepped back, because when I rubbed Jerrion's back he did not move at all. He did not even do the baby flinch (that little jump babies do when you touch them). At that moment, I picked him up only to see that he was not breathing. I ran to call for help, first 911 and then my family, to alert them as to what was going on. When the paramedics got there, I was hysterical and did the best that I could to report the night's events. The paramedic that was taking my report was trying to keep me focused so he could get all the information needed to assist me. He was very understanding and handled me with so much care and compassion. The other paramedic scooped my son up and rushed him out into the street, then into the ambulance. The entire time that I talked with the one paramedic, I could not take my eyes or attention off of the other; Thinking that my son's little life hung in the balance between this paramedics learned skills and my prayers. I was praying that he could bring my baby back. In the midst of the chaos, bottles still had to be made and I had to make sure the baby bag had all of the necessary items for travel. I still had another baby that I had to take care of. I wrapped Juston up and placed him in his carrier and by that time my family arrived to help escort us to the hospital.

I walked into that Emergency Room praying that my son was going to be okay. In my heart, I knew he was gone, but that did not stop me from hoping and praying. I was asking God to work a miracle. I remember being in a hallway when they gave me the news. First, I tried to wrap my mind around what they were telling me and then it felt like

I had been hit in the gut and then, came the emotional breakdown. My knees buckled, my body jolted, my arms and legs moved to fight whatever new level of hurt this was. I was picked up and carried to a room away from the ER nurses' station to give me and my family a moment to take in the horrific news that we had just received and grieve. I was still kicking and screaming and somehow ended up on the floor. Once I had calmed down and was off the floor, the nurse came in with tears rolling down her face. She was so sorry that amid my suffering, she still had to do her job and ask me questions that I was not sure how to even process. She sat next to me and looked me in my eyes and said, "I am so sorry, but I have to go over some paperwork with you." I had to discuss right then and there what funeral home my baby son would go to, sign an autopsy release form and a few other things that I was wishing I did not have to talk about at time; or at least I wish they could have waited until another time.

Two months to the day of his birth, my baby was pronounced dead at the hospital; cause of death, "SIDS". Nothing, I mean nothing on earth, can ever prepare you for this kind of loss. It was final! My son was gone! God had taken Jerrion into His loving arms of eternal rest.

When I left the hospital, I was numb. I felt like I was in a bad dream. I felt helpless and confused. I was now worried about Juston, "was the same thing going to happen to him? Was I going to have to go through this a second time?" Juston wore a heart monitor for a short time just as a safety precaution. After all, Juston was my sick baby at birth and my mind was all over the place. When your child dies it is the most gut-wrenching heartache you could ever go through. I questioned God with the normal why mine, why me, kinds of questions. I even blamed myself. I wondered what I could have done differently. The very foundation of my soul was shaken!

There I was having to plan a funeral for my baby. This entire process was torture for me. The planning, the picking of a casket (horrible melt down), programs and who was going to do what. When you have children, the plan is for them to bury you not the other way around. I felt like a zombie. I could see people talking but I could not hear their words, nor did I care about what they were saying. I was looking but not focused on any one thing. I just wanted it all to be over. Jerrion's service was graveside. It was nice and sweet, with family and friends attending. There was a song, a prayer and a few words of encouragement and talk about God's love and how he makes no mistakes. Well, honestly, at this point, I could not understand that. My precious baby boy was gone!

I was raised in a Pentecostal church, in Birmingham, Alabama, where my mother and stepfather pastored the church. I had sat in all the Sunday school classes, Bible studies, Friday night services, and Sunday morning and Sunday night services. Oh yeah, let's not forget about those weeklong revivals. So, I heard all the stories about God and his love, but at that moment I could not feel his love. I felt like my sins of adultery, fornication and lies had all come back to haunt me! I remember saying, "God is punishing me just like he did David and Bathsheba because of David's sins." I was without a relationship with God, so at the time I did not understand how God could love me so and still allow such pain to happen to me. How could He do this to me? How could He love me and take my precious baby boy? How???

When tragedy comes, people will also reference Job and how he lost everything he had and how he still trusted God. Or they tell you that God will not put more on you than you can bear. Although there is some truth to that, I did not want to hear any of it at this time. I felt like it did not apply to me. So, I had that conversation with God because I was mad. Yes, I was mad at God!!! I told Him, "Look I am NOT Job!" I cannot bare this. This is too much." But, the truth of the matter was, I had to bear it and go through it. My son was gone and there was nothing I could do about it. Nothing I could do would bring him back to me. I wondered many times why God choose my baby. I am not saying at all that any baby should die. But in my brokenness, I asked God "Why didn't you take some crackheads baby? Or one that would have problems for the rest of its life. Why did you take mine? I was going to love him and do right by him." But, truthfully, the answer to the whys may never come in an audible voice from God. I could not spend my time wondering about things that I didn't know. It was my own soul that I needed to be concerned about. I needed to make sure that I did what I was supposed to do so that one day when my name is called, I will also rest in him forever just like my baby boy. I could have beat my head up against a steel wall and asked why from then until eternity and still not get a clear answer. I just had to know that it was not my fault and there was nothing I could have done to prevent his death. Sometimes what we suffer is a direct result of our actions and sometimes it's not. The bible talks about the good and the bad suffering the same and it rains on the just as well as the unjust. Sometimes bad things just happen to good people.

My return to church for the most part, was comforting until I encountered this sister at the church. It was during offering time and we had placed our offering in the pan at the altar. When I turned around, she was standing there. "Praise the Lord. How are you?" she asked. I started to make conversation with her about my baby dying and before I could complete my sentence she said, "Now you know how God felt when Jesus died on the cross". She rolled her eyes and walked away. I will never forget what she said to me. I was a 20-year-old young adult who was fragile in spirit. I walked away and took my seat. I sat there in shame, not really knowing how to feel about what she said to me. In that moment she failed to show me Gods love, which is what I needed at the time and not her judgment.

Love is one of God's attributes and an essential part of his nature. What I had to realize is that God loved me and all the stories that I had heard at church were just that, examples of what happens to mankind. They did not become alive to me until I developed my own personal relationship with God. Then I understood His love for me. I think my son came into my life for a brief moment to be the vessel that God would use for my journey to salvation. It did not happen right away. It took about three years before I completely surrendered my heart to the Lord. There came a day when I had come to myself and knew that there was no way my heart could be healed without my Creator. I knocked and the door was opened. I sought Him and He found me. I asked Him to come into my heart and He did. Then I learned the length, width and depth of his love. I had to come to peace with the fact that my baby was in heaven and that he was being loved by the only one who could love him better than me. Heaven is also my destination, a place I want to go. It's like David said concerning his beloved son "I will go to him." In other words, I will surely see him one day.

Through the years, I have had some unexpected moments of upset. One time I was in a CPR class and had a "straight come apart' when it was time to perform the infant CPR portion of the course. It was so bad they had to give me special accommodations to finish the course. I had a wave of emotions that came up and out from nowhere; I thought I was good. I thought I had gotten past all of that. At that point, it had been about six years since my son passed away. Sometimes tragedy and devastation can cut you so deeply that it takes time for healing to take place. Some scars will heal and fade in no time not even leaving a trace that they had been there. My scars are not physical they are mental and emotional. When I raised my other three boys, I lived in fear of something happening to them and truthfully, sometimes it is still a struggle. Fear was always somewhere lurking in the back of my mind. It is my relationship with God that keeps me focused and sane. I have to constantly pray for them and know that God's got them.

Every year around the month of August I go through what they call anniversary grief. This does not happen because I want it to, for me it is more subconscious. There are times when it will hit me like a freight train and other times it is very subtle. I don't have to be thinking about my son or his death, but it just happens. Sometimes, it catches me by surprise, and I try to shake it off. During these times I try to keep busy, go visit family or friends, worship (it works for me) or try to be in some kind of positive head space. I do whatever I can to not be depressed. Then there are times when nothing helps and I have learned to be OK with that too. There is no timeline to the grief process because we all grieve differently.

I lost my son five days after my birthday, so the joy of celebrating is not always there when that time rolls around. So sometimes it takes the initiation of someone else for me to celebrate. One year was really bad and I could feel the depression train coming. I could hear the horn blow, feel the earth moving and I could see the smoke. I don't know what makes one year worse than the other. This one particular year, I had a friend that wanted to celebrate me every day for a whole week. She was so excited about my birthday, way more excited than I was. She was running down all the things we were going to do every day for the week of my birthday. What she did not realize, was that God was using her to save me from the biggest depression storm ever. Every day I looked forward to whatever we were going to do together. It wasn't until sometime later that I shared with her how what she did helped me. She never knew I was having anniversary grief, most people don't. It is not something I talk much about.

For many years, I have suffered in silence, partly because I felt like if I did not talk about it, it would make the hurt go away. I did not have anyone close to me who hand lost a baby that could understand how I felt and could be sensitive to my feelings. I did not attend counseling to sort out my feelings, which would have probably been beneficial for me. I have learned that the effects of trauma and the residue it leaves behind is real and that trusting God to see you through is great and should be first and foremost, but talking to a professional can be also helpful through your grieving process.

When I think of the son I lost twenty-three years ago, I smile. I don't really cry anymore or haven't for some time now. When I look at Juston, who is a man now, I wonder what Jerrion would have looked like. I sometimes wonder if they would have been the type twins of that were joined at the hip or if they would have been very different. When all of this happened, people gave me all kinds of explanations, whether learned or hearsay like: "It's always the healthy twin that dies" or "the babies just forget how to breathe." For many years I held onto these words to give me a reason and to make sense of why this happened. In doing my own studies, some researchers suggest that some babies have sleep apnea. Sleep apnea is a sleep disorder which causes pausing in breathing or periods of shallow breathing occur while you are asleep. I cannot at this point be certain of what really happened to my son, but sleep apnea is not at all far-fetched being almost my entire family has been diagnosed with it: myself, my mother, my brother, my uncle, and my great aunt to name a few. I remember when I had my doctors' visit. The doctor drew a diagram to show me what a normal airway looked like and then he showed me mine. He said that I had an abnormal airway and Thank God my brain does what it was supposed to do and wakes me up or I would suffocate to death. SIDS (Sudden Infant Death Syndrome), also known as "crib death", is a sudden unexplained death of a child less than one year old. Research is still being done to find the cause of infant deaths. In honor of my son, I am dedicated to supporting SIDS research to advance the studies to find out why our babies die. It is my prayer that one day we will have some understanding.

At the end of the day, no matter what I have gone through, I have learned to trust God with everything. He is the lover of my soul, my hiding place and where I can run and be safe. I don't always understand what He does or why He allows some things to be so, but I know He is GOD and holds all power in His hands. He is the potter, and I am the clay. He is the salve for every wound. So, for now, I will keep this prayer close to my heart. "God grant me the serenity to accept the things I cannot change, the courage to change the things I can and the wisdom to know the difference."

Jerrilyn Harris is a native of Alabama currently residing in Snellville, Georgia. She is a woman of faith, a true worshipper and sings in the choir. Jerrilyn is the mother of 3 sons, but knows the tragedy of losing a child. She worked at the Department of the Army for many years, but now serves as an Executive Administrative Assistant in the medical industry. She is also involved in multiple small business ventures which have allowed her to become a more passionate supporter of SIDS research. She enjoys crafting and traveling. She is now investigating her ancestry and hopes to one day travel to Africa.

CHAPTER 4

SHAPED AND MOLDED BY
THE HAND OF GOD
SHARON AYTCH HARRIS

I was child in Waterbury, Maryland. An athletic child, the only girl on Baltimore Hill Road, nicknamed by my great Uncle Jim," Bell Starr," a tough cowgirl/woman in Westerns. I ruled my boy cousins, I could hit the ball harder, run faster, and cussed like sailor at age 8.

I felt the hand of God for the first time when I was that eight-year-old athletic child.

I was climbing a tree, and always one to show off; I climbed higher than my male cousin. I climbed about 15 feet that day. I had not discovered the spirit of fear yet, my innocent heart still remembered who I was.

As I was laughing and taunting my cousin, suddenly the branch that I was sitting on broke. I was headed to fall into a gulley full of fallen trees, broken glass bottles and rocks thrown into the gulley by me and my cousins. However, while I was falling, the last branch before I fell into the gulley seemed to have reached out to catch me, I grabbed ahold to the branch, with my little eight-year-old feet dangling, I pulled myself up and whispered, "Thank you God for catching me." That day I knew there was a God.

A year later my father was killed, a pedestrian struck by a car; me and my five-year-old brother were the last two people to see him alive.

That rainy-day February 1973 it had rained most of the day, it finally stopped around 3pm in the afternoon. My grandmother sent me to the neighborhood store

"Meade's" at the bottom of Baltimore Hill Road and General Highway, with her shopping list.

I was excited to go to the store because I had my own agenda. My plan was to get a five cent bottle of Coca-Cola, and a ten cent bag of chips; and with my, "car loving," little brother in tow, we would sit on the crates in the side parking lot and watch the teenage boys spin donuts in their Chevy Nova's. But, when I entered the store much to my surprise, there stood my father, grocery bag in hand, happy to see us he handed me the bag of groceries.

He had gotten off from work early; picked up the items my grandmother needed and hustled us back out of the store.

You should have seen my little pissed off face (hiding from my father). Little did he know he had thrown a monkey wrench in my plans. Damn!

He instructed me to take the grocery bag home because he was going across the road to see his sister, Aunt Catherine and he would see us at home in an hour.

As my little brother and I headed back up the hill and around the bend headed for home, we heard a car with loud screeching and tires squealing. My little brother looked up at me and said, "Let's go back and watch the teenagers do donuts in the parking lot." We turned and started back, but I was stopped in my tracks with a gut feeling of despair. I told my brother, "No, we better get these groceries home because daddy will be angry if we go back to the lot and he sees us."

An hour later, my 32-year-old father was dead leaving his wife, and five children, ages 9, 7, 5, 2, and 1. This was my second time feeling the hand of God. "Thank You God, for urging me to take my brother home!"

Five years later, it is December 1977, and I am pregnant.

I am 14 years old and I am revealing to my grandmother that I am pregnant. I am afraid to tell my mother. My mom disconnected a little after losing my father, so my grandmother became "my person," my confidant, so I left it up to her to break this news to my mother.

As my mother and grandmother gathered to discuss me and my situation, as if I am not in the room, my mother schedules a doctor's appointment.

My pediatrician, nurse practitioner Warner, breaks the news, "its official she's pregnant!" Nurse Practitioner Warner and my mother make plans, again as if I weren't in the room, to terminate the pregnancy.

When my mother and I get home, my mother informs my grandmother of the results, of yes, she is pregnant, and she is getting an abortion (something I never agreed on).

That night I slept with my grandmother, and as I tossed and turned, cried, and prayed. This time I cried out for the presence of God I cried out for Him and said. "Help me God, I cannot abort this baby."

That morning I told my grandmother, "I am an "A" student, I am not a statistic and I refuse to be labeled! I cannot abort this baby!!"

We together stood firm against my mothers' wishes and the summer of my 9th grade year, I was the mother of a 6lbs, 9oz baby boy, born August 19, 1978.

I did not miss a day of school during my pregnancy and I continued to be an honor student. I started my sophomore year with my class in September of 1978. Thank God for my grandmother, she was my saving grace. When the baby would awaken at 2 a.m., she would have me bring her the baby so I would be able to rest and make it to school the next day. My grandmother's "GRACE" was remarkable! There was no way I could have muddled through without her.

I was a full-time student, I worked part time and I was a mother of an infant child. When exhaustion settled in as I questioned my decision to raise a child, as I was little more than a child myself, my grandmother would keep me focused and often remind me that I was special and I had a job to do; And that job, was to be the best I could be for that child. She constantly reminded me that God would not give me more than I could handle. I was not trying to hear that, and I didn't hear God! I had placed God in the back seat of my life and damnit I am tired!

I was tired but stubborn because I was determined not to be a welfare recipient, high school dropout, teenage mother. I worked hard, awfully hard, and I graduated with my class June of 1981.

That same summer, I witnessed many of my friends becoming addicted to drugs and alcohol. While they were partying, I was home with my baby. I would sit on the front step late at night on Royal Street with not a soul in sight. My friends were gone, off to "Honey Comb Hideout", a party house that summer.

I was always old for my age. My close friends called me "Momma"... I was always busy. I'm a mother, and I'm only 17 years old.

I wanted to go to the "Y", I wanted to go to the Stanton Center" and dance to "Le Freak" by Chic. Both the "Y", and "Stanton Center" were local hangout places in Annapolis. But what I discovered, and so appreciate today, was that baby saved my life. "Thank you, God, for that child."

My senior year of high school I worked for Anne Arundel County District Court as a court recorder, and that's where I met Mr. Reggie, the Courtroom Bailiff.

Mr. Reggie was highly respected, as he was one of Maryland's first black State Troopers. He had a presence of authority about him that commanded the courtroom; he was very intimidating and a little scary.

On downtime, Mr. Reggie was a delight to work with. He would tease me about hooking me up with his son. With much skepticism, I would tease him back suggesting that he make it happen and pinky swear I would go out with him. Just let me know, I'd tell him, when and where. We'd go back and forth about him hooking me up with his son for months. I never really took him serious; we would laugh and go on about our courtroom business.

That same summer in 1981 I had a crush on a guy from the neighborhood. I would watch him play basketball and daydream (I am a Pisces) about hanging out with him. He also was an amateur DJ, so he'd spin the records at our Youth Community Center (also known as the Rec). He paid me NO attention.

But being from the neighborhood I was friends with his sisters, so, I spent a lot of time with them hoping to attract his attention. His middle sister invited me to attend her wedding. I was excited, here was a chance for me to hang out with her brother, and I accepted! It was a beautiful wedding. There were many people that attended whom I didn't know, so I stayed close to the sisters as they mingled with their guests.

At some point, I engaged into a conversation with the bride regarding an upcoming event she was hosting, and she asked if I would like to attend. I declined, stating I wouldn't have a date and I was not attending alone. Overhearing our conversation this handsome man says, "I'll take you".

Side- eyed, I replied, "Thank you, but I do not know you." The Bride laughed and introduced us. She told me that he was a co-worker and a nice guy. I hesitated, but finally agreed to allow him to take me to the event. You know what they say about wedding and funerals; you just might meet "THE ONE".

Mr. Marvin Harris took me to the event, then to the movies, then out to dinner at a restaurant with linen tablecloths (that was fancy for me at that age) and then skiing. At the time, I'm thinking, "I didn't know black People skied!"

He was quickly becoming my best friend.

He fell in love with my son, now 3 years old, and my son loved him. My mom, grandmother and siblings all fell for Mr. Marvin Harris. Marvin was 10 years older than me, but I could hold a conversation with him about anything; After all, remember I was an honor student, well read and confident. These were the days before Google, so I had to actually read books. Marvin nurtured our relationship far longer than I did. He took care of me and my child. He was my soft place to land. He was my "waiting to exhale".

About four months into dating Marvin he told me that his grandmother was battling cancer. On this particular Sunday afternoon, his father requested that he and his siblings come to their home. Marvin asked if I would go with him. When we arrived his family members were all upstairs, he directed me to the living room, and I walked to the fireplace to admire the family photos cluttered along the mantel. And to my surprise, I recognized a face; I discovered Marvin's father is...

WAIT FOR IT...

Mr. REGGIE!!! God was sending Marvin into my life long before I met him! Mr. Reggie came downstairs and saw me standing there and said, "I knew you were the one for my son". Eight years later, we married on June 8, 1989. "Thank you God for this man."

I never got into the drug and alcohol scene like many of my peers. When I was 13, my friends were already smoking weed. My older god brothers, five and six years my senior, always had weed. They played in a local band; my family was a musical family. My father was a bass guitar player, and my mother was a singer. So, when my god brothers played gigs at the local Community Youth Center, I was allowed to attend if they kept an eye on me.

This night as the band members were setting up the equipment, the lead female singer walked outside alone. It was dark, I didn't really know her, but she was from the neighborhood and when you're from the neighborhood, you're family. So, I walked out behind her to keep her company.

She walked along the side of the building and lit a joint (weed). She passed it to me, and I took it. I am about to have my first encounter smoking weed.

I drew in the smoke, inhaled and smoked it with her until it was done. We walked back inside the building, the band members were still setting up and then, it hit me. I was HIGH!!!

I thought I was going to lose my mind. I cried out and startled my god brothers, so they came running to my assistance. Confused as to what was wrong with me, crying out, I told them "I smoked a joint and I'm scared!!"

The fear in their eyes was something I will never forget. I demanded to go to the ER (emergency room. I thought my heart was pounding through my chest. I was paranoid. I cried when they refused to take me; trying to rationalize with me they told me if they took me to the ER we would all be in trouble.

I hated that feeling of severe paranoia, I felt as if I was on the brink of a psychotic break. They took me to the car, took turns caring for me in shifts until I began to feel better. I never touched weed again after that night. "Thank you, God, for getting me through that night."

Cocaine use and addiction ran through our community like wildfire in the early 90's, and my husband became a victim; he battled with cocaine addiction for decades. He put at risk all of his relationships and ruined some.

With my son in the backseat of my car I am banging on strangers' doors in the middle of the night tracking down my husband, hoping to bring him home. He would go missing for days and gone with him was his paycheck.

Struggling to pay the bills and Marvin missing important

family engagements, I'm trying to cover for him. I thought I would lose my mind for the second time in my life, this time through being married and loving an addict.

My world went dark during those years. I didn't feel God, I was angry with God, and I was done with God and Marvin.

How could either of them love me and put me through this nightmare? My heart was in pain, I was mentally exhausted, and I didn't know where to turn. I wanted to be disconnected to everything and just go numb.

I was struggling alone with Marvin's addiction, and I was tired with covering for him, and hiding his secret from family and friends. Finally, in 1992, I left Marvin.

I was all five letters C.R.A.Z.Y during that time. I faked happy, I faked smiles. I was unhappy with him, and I was unhappy without him. I could not feel God's presence at all. I just felt numb. I was living day to day, just pushing through the days. I was surviving not thriving, just going through the motions, so I decided to go back to church.

I had stopped going to church in my early twenties, but I felt a pull to return. I joined the choir. I participated in ministries, but my household was still a mess. Marvin and I would get back together, he would start using again. Then, we would separate again. As family and friends began to discover Marvin was an addict, the pressure on me got harder.

Paranoid that our family would think I was also battling

with cocaine I gained weight on purpose because crackheads are thin, so I picked up the weight to distance myself from my husband and any community rumors. Lord have mercy, I am losing my mind.

I prayed that God would take the desire of cocaine from my husband. I was angry and frustrated all the time. I lost respect for the love of my life, and I wanted it all to just to STOP.

Please God, stop the world so I can get off. I definitely wasn't enjoying this ride or the scenery. Depression and suicidal thoughts lingered like a dark cloud during those years. However, I needed to live and keep pushing because of my son. He was my reason for living and he needed me. Thank you, God, for that child!

The spirit of addiction is real, and many suffer in silence. I began to change my prayer, as I prayed to God to show me how to support my husband, I remembered the Grace granted to me by my grandmother as I struggled being a teenage mother. I had to remember and had to show my husband that very same Grace.

My heart opened and I began to share my struggles, and some really great people allowed me to talk as they listened.

There was no judgment from these living Angels, as they helped me reconnect with the Savior, and showed me that I was not alone. They prayed with me and for me, I will never forget them.

First Christian Community Church of Annapolis was a place of security, peace and joy for me during that time, and the Deacon couple assigned to me loved me and took care of my broken heart. Lead by the late Pastor Richard Johnson III, they helped me to see things from a different perspective. They assured me that I was not alone in my struggles. I learned from them the importance of fellowship and of surrounding yourself with true people of God.

"For our struggle is not against flesh and blood, but against the rulers against the authorities, against the powers of this dark world and against the spiritual forces of evil in the heavenly realms..." Ephesians 6:12

I was reminded I have a friend in Jesus, and I remembered the guidance of The Holy Spirit and God reminded me of His Grace.

June 8, 2020 Marvin and I celebrated 39 years together (31 of those celebrated as husband and wife). He's sober and free of the bondage of cocaine addiction. Together we have raised two awesome boys to men and are currently living our best life.

What I have learned and I am thrilled to share is, God has been with me my entire life, putting me through the fires of my experiences, as he molded and created me into the person that I am today.

I may have put Him in the backseat, but He placed Himself in the front seat of my heart and soul.

I now understand that my struggles and the darkness in my life, was my personal version of being on the cross.

I may have suffered, but I endured. One day at a time became my motto and today I live my full purpose in this life. My full purpose is to always strive to be a blessing to all who crosses my path.

Through my life experiences, I was created to be a good listener, I learned to humble myself and check myself so that I may be a blessing to others. *"Maneuver in Love Always"* is my morning mantra.

If you need a shoulder to cry on or just an ear just to be heard, I am here for you. My "Big Chair" is always available. (People who know me know exactly what I'm talking about). I can tell you, keep living, and keep learning as this too shall pass. Most importantly grasp the fact that you are not alone.

Teenage pregnancy is not the end. Drug addiction is not the end. Depression and suicidal thoughts are   real, but it's not the end!

Triumph awaits! God introduced himself to me at the age of eight and he never left my side. My feet are still dangling, but not because of a fall it is now because with Him, I am sitting atop the world!

Thank you, God, for teaching me Grace.

Thank you, God, for my everyday peace, joy and happiness.

Thank you, God, for my family and friends, their love and support.

Thank you, God, just because!

Sharon Aytch Harris lives in Metro Atlanta with her husband of 31 years, son, nephew and two exceptionally perfect dogs. Sharon was born and raised in Annapolis, Maryland. The eldest of five siblings along with being a teenage mother, leadership came natural to her. Sharon is a Health Administrator managing a Geriatric Psychiatry Program, diagnosing and treatment of many dementias including Alzheimer's disease and other mood disorders. Sharon loves good food, fun and the comfort of her close-knit inner circle of friends and family. Sharon also has a love of all genres of music and she is an avid reader with a vivid imagination. One of Sharon's favorite quotes is ..."God is great, Beer is good, and people are crazy". (Billy Currington)

Thank you for your support Sylvia, and I look forward to reading your story !! :)

CHAPTER 5

BETTER THAN I DESERVED
WIL WILLIAMSON

I am a Chaplain.

My friend and fellow insurance entrepreneur Jim Somers and I would meet on occasion for lunch in Atlanta, Georgia, and during our conversations and reflections on our success in the industry, he would always ask me how I am doing, and I would always respond, "Better than I deserved, Jim."

I always knew, even as a small boy, that I wanted to help people; spiritually or financially, in some capacity or the other. So, I dedicated the past 26 years of my training to becoming an insurance professional. It worked!

Life was good, my career was moving on an upward trajectory, even after a marital split in 2014 and an unexpected loss of my mother in 2017. Those were some trying times in my life. Thank God for my family, my church and friends who helped me get through those seasons of grief.

Have you ever received some news that gave you an out of body experience? Some news that literally rocked your world?

"We need to have a video conference," said Dr. Levey, my primary care physician from Kaiser Permanente. Seven days earlier, I had a complete physical and a biopsy to check my prostate because of a higher than normal PSA reading. I logged onto my patient physician portal and to access my telehealth visit with my physician. During the video conference, Dr. Levey recommended I come in to see him in person, to discuss the results of my physical exam and my biopsy. At this point, all sorts of thoughts went through my head. "Why did he want me to come in? Why couldn't he just tell me now?" I couldn't get an appointment with him two weeks because of the pandemic. I'm sure you can understand the unanswered questions I had. It must be serious because he wanted to see me personally in the middle of a pandemic.

Two weeks later, I arrived at Kaiser. After having my temperature checked at the door and donning my mask, I walked into Dr. Levey's office and sat down on his green chair that he had set up for his patients. "You have signs of stage II prostate cancer," he said, in a soft low tone. I replied: "Ok Doc, tell me what I need to do." If I wasn't devastated enough by that news, I became more devastated about the treatments and the side effects of those treatments which he explained to me that I would have to undergo to eradicate the cancer. I immediately thought of my three sons, my uncle, who passed away from this same cancer in 2000, my family – what would they think? How did I get this? What would my employees do? Who would run the corporation if I passed? Then, I suddenly felt this "out of body feeling" and in my mind just a few questions to God--- why me? And why now?

Dr. Levey then told me to take four weeks and think about the options of radiation or surgery and let him know my decision. Radiation treatment, he said, would create the inability for me to have more children; it would compromise my immune system and could cause ED (erectile dysfunction) among other things. Having the surgery would remove the entire prostate, which is 99% more effective. I would, however, need round the clock care for the next four weeks or so. I knew I didn't have the latter option. As COVID-19 was resurging and I did not want to be away from my office for that long. I knew right then and there that radiation treatments and the brachytherapy was my best bet. Brachytherapy is a procedure that involves placing radioactive material inside your body. Brachytherapy is one type of radiation therapy that's used to treat cancer.

The next few weeks would challenge my faith and mortality, open some doors of trust and create this whirlwind I could never have imagined.

I remember texting my sister Kaye, and my siblings and then calling my father in the Bronx, New York to give him the news of my diagnosis; he then disclosed to me something I never knew- He explained to me that he had been living with an enlarged prostate for many, many years. In that moment, I believed that God wanted me not to feel alone in this journey and gave me the answer to one of my many questions. Two days later, I received a call from my friend, Mike; he too was at the tail end of his treatments and wished me well. We shared about the great fellowships we had at the church back in the day and the willingness to beat this disease soon. God has His way of letting us know that we are not alone.

In late August 2020, I was referred to Emory Hospital at the Winship Cancer Institute in Sandy Springs GA to begin my six weeks of radiation treatments and "seed surgery" or brachytherapy. That day when I pulled up to that Cancer Institute, it finally hit me, I was diagnosed with stage II prostate cancer and there was no time to waste! After arriving walking a few minutes from the purple deck parking lot, I was greeted at the door by the screeners asking if I had a cough, fevers or if I had been exposed to or tested for COVID-19 lately? My answer was "No". About 30 minutes later, while sitting in the lobby, I heard my name being called. I was greeted by two male nurses, as they escorted me to the back, they explained to me what to expect during the treatment, the procedures and the duration of the treatment; then I was taken to the room when I would be residing for the next six weeks. Since the radiation will go into points in the area of the prostate, there had to be "tattoo-like" markings on my body to help facilitate that. Therefore, I had to take all of my clothes off to get this done and take showers carefully, so as not to remove these markings.

Dr. Patel, the chief oncologist, met me at the conclusion of my first treatment in his office and warmly introduced himself with a fist bump, to make me feel at ease. "I will be your doctor for your surgery," he said. "I promise you that I and the staff, will take great care of you, and I will meet with you every Friday at the end of the week to see your progress." So, every day, for the next six weeks, my journey started to eradicate this cancer from my body.

One Saturday, one of my customers (we will call her "P"), randomly telephoned me to find out how I was doing, when I told her my diagnosis, she started to cry. She was expressing how cruel life can be, but within the hour, she had sent me some homemade chicken soup, a few bottles of cranberry juices and some coconut water to help, she says, with the "healing process". I needed that example of care and compassion for what was about to happen to me next.

Two weeks into my radiation treatments, I suffered bouts of fatigue, nausea, and dizziness. The nurse from Kaiser Permanente called me to come in for a shot to help with some pain I had been suffering in my wrist for quite some time. I went there immediately following my radiation treatment. That Wednesday afternoon, I was faced with my own mortality. As the kind nurse administered the shot, it felt like hard pinch. She asked me if I was ok, I replied "yes", but suddenly I started losing consciousness, my blood pressure dropped and my eyes rolled to the back of my head; As I started slowly falling to the floor, I heard someone yell for help! I saw and felt myself falling, like in the movie "Get Out" just drifting away. "Put some ice on his neck," someone yelled. "Get his legs above his head," yelled another. "Tell me your name and date of birth?" yelled yet another.

For what seemed an eternity for me ended after ten

minutes, as I gingerly responded and slowly came back to consciousness. Those nurses brought me back! Those were angels in my life!

The day of the Brachytherapy "seed surgery", this is where they put needles in my prostate to try and shrink it, the anesthesiologist and Dr. Patel stopped by my bed, and assured me that I would not feel a thing. I noticed they never said, "See you when you get through." They never do. But I told my family and friends, that I would see them on the other side of through.

I was in surgery for six hours. As they took me to recovery, I was experiencing a lot of discomfort, slight pains and blood was all over my bed, which they said was normal. But, most importantly, the surgery was deemed a success! The days and weeks ahead were challenging. Sitting was painful. Getting to the bathroom was a show of true grit. Urinating had never been more excruciating, and the simple act of eating became a chore. The combination of Ibuprofen and Flomax medications made my days annoying, to say the least. I was in a perpetual state of fatigue, exhaustion and grogginess.

Then, there was a time, emotionally, when I questioned, "Could this be my lifestyle now?" Like, wearing male pampers everywhere I go. I certainly could not dream of my life being this way. I'm a chaplain, remember? I said, "How am I going to encourage others when I need help myself?" I had to reflect on the goodness and graciousness of God. I still considered myself a fighter and this was only a temporary journey to a place of healing and restoration.

If there's anything this cancer experience has taught me is the appreciation for life. I saw my daily radiation treatments as the impetus for taking care of myself. I'm usually that kind of a guy anyway, "A SELF-CARE GUY", but during this period I listened to more music and audio books, Joel Osteen, Les Brown and Zig Ziglar just to name a few; especially while I drove myself to treatments. However, the final two weeks I was so fatigued I took UBER daily. Both of those methods of inspiration became calming and soothing rituals for me. I laughed and shared more with my staff and family, and I gave myself permission to do what I needed to do and never worried about the things I could not and cannot control.

If you, or anyone you know has a cancer diagnosis, please share and practice these several important life lessons as I have. Keep the people you love very close and keep them informed. Learn how to live, love and enjoy each and every day, because each day is truly a gift from God. Take time for yourself and spend as much time as you can with the ones you love because they will be there through the worse.

Even though my treatment is complete, my fight against cancer is not. I now have to learn how to balance love, life and live. I now also want to find a way to help the survivors of prostate cancer and that has started with me sharing my experience in this book. In 2021, through my non-profit, I purpose to help educate, elevate and rejuvenate the survivors of prostate cancer, especially men of color, as this disease affects us more than any other group. I cannot stress enough to my African American brothers the importance to get checked annually for prostate cancer after the age of 40. It could save your life.

I know that God is still in the healing business and I have truly gained a new appreciation for LIFE. Why? Because I was given "Better Than I Deserved."

For over a decade, Allstate Insurance Company agency owner **Wil Williamson** has been a business leader and an involved citizen in the Tucker/Stone Mountain Georgia area. In September 2007, he started THE WILLIAMSON INSURANCE GROUP, Inc. He has earned numerous awards and designations with the company for his outstanding financial knowledge and personal customer service experience. His drive and love for helping others is wrapped up in one of his favorite quotes from his mentor, the late Zig Ziglar, "Help enough people get what they want, then you will get what you want." As an ordained minister and Chaplain, he recognizes all of his gifts and blessings are from God and are to be shared with the world. He enjoys volunteering with "Meals on Wheels Atlanta", cycling, traveling and golfing when permissible. He is also a published author. His first book was released in 2018 entitled, "Informed and Insured".